Journal

Your Way To
A Peaceful World

LIVE LIKE YOU WANT IT; YOU HAVE A
ROLE; YOUR HAPPINESS MATTERS

JOAN MARIE GAGNON

BALBOA.
PRESS

A DIVISION OF HAY HOUSE

"Physician, heal thyself" (Luke 4:23).

Balboa Press books may be ordered through booksellers or by contacting:

Balboa Press
A Division of Hay House
1663 Liberty Drive
Bloomington, IN 47403
www.balboapress.com
1 (877) 407-4847

ISBN: 978-1-5043-9171-9 (sc)
ISBN: 978-1-5043-9172-6 (e)

Library of Congress Control Number: 2017917650

Print information available on the last page.

Balboa Press rev. date: 11/27/2017

Dedicated to my loving husband,
James D. Goyea,
who combines sensitivity and logic like no other.

Preface

If you picked up this book, you are probably as sad and concerned about our world as I am. I sometimes wonder if we would be better off without the Internet and immediate access to world news, but I immediately discount this idea quickly. Don't we need to know what is happening in the world so we can help change the negative things and celebrate the good ones? I continually bounce back and forth about whether or not to go off the grid for a week from the regular feed of news and tweets. Can you relate to this seesaw?

This workbook is designed to help us connect with God, the universe, the earth, and our fellow humans throughout the world. As we become more peaceful within ourselves, this peace will radiate out to the world. We will explore the meaning of *unconditional love* with the goal of knowing and feeling it as well as other emotions we may have ignored in the past, which are relevant to peace in our world.

My favorite authors and teachers are Fr. Richard Rohr, Dr. Joe Dispenza, and Gregg Braden. Through a combination of their teachings, we will explore science, spirituality, and ancestral knowledge. We will be touching on these modalities throughout this workbook so we can all work together to bring peace to our world.

Dr. Joe Dispenza received his doctor of chiropractic degree from Life University, graduating with honors. His postgraduate training covered neurology, neuroscience, brain function, chemistry, cellular biology, memory formation, and aging and longevity. Gregg Braden is an internationally renowned author and speaker, as well as a pioneer in bridging science, spirituality, and the real world. Fr. Richard Rohr is a globally recognized ecumenical teacher who bears witness to the universal awakening within Christian mysticism. He is a Franciscan priest of the New Mexico Province and founder of the Center for Action and Contemplation in Albuquerque, New Mexico.

I want to be clear that I am not a spiritual teacher or a therapist. I am a researcher, a writer, and a wannabe activist. In my chapter "For Further Reading," I have provided many references to materials and books, which expand on some of the topics discussed in this book.

Journaling is an excellent way to gather your thoughts on a subject and to bring clarity. Don't let that carping voice inside convince you that journaling is useless and a waste of time. I will provide you with journaling tips along the way. Hey, if you don't want to journal, that is okay too. Dwell, pray, or meditate on the subject at hand. Any of these activities lead us to a more peaceful world. You may even find yourself jumping over chapters and even questions within them. That is fine. Go with what inspires you at that moment.

The first chapter will give you suggestions on how to utilize this book. So let's get to it.

Contents

Introduction

How to Utilize This Book

> *Things do not happen. Things are made to happen.*
>
> *—John F. Kennedy*

Attitude and Intention

Your attitude and intention around these journal questions matter greatly to truly connect with the intent of the book. You can utilize the space in this book or purchase a beautiful spiral-bound journal to set the tone of you being serious about this journey.

Journaling your thoughts can bring up feelings that have an impact on your being. As you journal your way through these questions, be prepared to feel calm, joyful, ecstatic, sad, mad, and, sometimes, overwhelmed.

These emotions may then make their way into your physical being. For instance, if you are writing about something that makes you angry, you might end up with a stomachache. Don't give up if these physical symptoms occur. I mention this to you now because, subconsciously, you may stop journaling when it seems you always get a headache or stomachache during or after your writing session. This is normal. Persevere.

Some of the journal questions may be thought provoking and conjure up some old memories or fears. If they do then yay! The journaling is working.

Date Your Journaling

It will be interesting to see how things change after a few weeks or months of journaling. It will be fascinating, in the months to come, not only to witness changes in your own life but also in those who surround you—as well as positive changes in the world. It will be great to see the progress you've made and how writing has given you the clarity to make your life more peaceful. You will be able to see and to celebrate this progress.

How Often Should You Journal?

How often you journal is up to you. Some people will want to plow through the book while others will want to contemplate each question for a week. I recommend you test it out for yourself. For example, if you answer one question per day but are still thinking about it three questions later, it might make sense to slow down a bit.

Exercises/Meditations

Each chapter has extra writing space, which is located at the end of the book starting on page 90. Use this if you need more space. I've included some guided meditations so you can go deeper starting on page 125. The litmus test is an excellent tool to utilize for the rest of your life, especially if you are making an important decision.

If you aren't sure about journaling, try the weekly Sticky Note Journaling Series exercises in Chapter 11 starting on page 117.

Chapter 1

The Power of Journaling

I want to write, but more than that, I want to bring out

all kinds of things that lie buried deep in my heart.

—Anne Frank

Since the late 1970s, neurological scientists have been discussing the functions of the left (logical) and right (creative) hemispheres of the brain. What if we were able to use the whole brain at the same time?

Brain research is fascinating. I could spend days reading about it. It turns out that we use both sides of the brain for all functions. I have spent a lot of time studying about the power of putting pen to paper and utilizing the whole brain. It takes *both* sides of the brain to be logical or to be creative. The act of writing is a function of one side of your brain, but the opposite side chooses the best word. So you can't have one without the other. Hence, we use the whole brain when journaling.

Handwriting itself is a very complex brain function for human beings, compared to other functions like walking or moving your toes. A lot of brain space is devoted to the use of fingers and hands. Therefore, it stands to reason that handwriting and putting pen to paper stimulate the brain. How good is that? Do you write by hand much these days? We are so quick to use the computer.

According to <u>Psych Central</u>, there is increasing evidence that journaling has a positive impact on physical well-being. James Pennebaker, a University of Texas at Austin psychologist and researcher, contends that regular journaling strengthens immune cells called T lymphocytes.[1]

What Other Benefits Do We Derive from Journaling?

Journaling Exposes Jumbled Thoughts

The Cleveland Clinic's website has stated that the average person has sixty thousand thoughts per day. Wow! Those are a lot of thoughts. It is important to know that our thoughts are not facts. It would be a very scary world if they were. The benefit of journaling for twenty minutes or so a day is that we are able to take those thoughts, bring them into the present, and analyze them without passion. We can question those thoughts. We can take control of those thoughts, whether they are positive or negative. How powerful is that?

Journaling Helps You Love Yourself

When you journal on a routine basis, one day you notice, *Gee, I feel happy.* One of my journaling habits is to write five things I am grateful for in that particular moment. It takes me about two minutes to do that exercise. My grateful items can be as intense as a resolved business issue or as everyday as the fact I have a heated house on a frigid morning.

Let's start now. What five things are you grateful for today?

Date:_____

_____

_____

_____

_____

_____

Journaling Can Reduce Stress

As I mentioned previously, we have potentially sixty thousand thoughts per day. Do you think they are all positive? I would guess *not*. When we journal about things that make us mad or sad, it calms us down for the present moment. This calmness creates positive hormones for our bodies. It also helps us stay in the present. Remember, our thoughts are not facts.

Journaling Can Help Solve Problems and Help You Understand Another Person's Perspective

Write a story from his or her perspective. I have used this exercise often, and it has produced a calmness and has given me understanding regarding a perceived problem with another person. Before I started journaling, I would stew over an issue for days, weeks, and yes, years before letting something go.

Okay, so you may have gathered by now that journaling can have a positive impact on our lives. This is great for us, right? But guess what, it helps world peace too.

Chapter 2

I'm Connected to You?

> *A mind that is stretched to a new idea never*
>
> *returns to its original dimension.*
>
> —*Oliver Wendell Holmes*

Science is now proving what mystics have known for centuries. We are all connected. Humans, animals, the earth, our deceased, etc. are all connected. What I think and do impacts my neighbor, my dog, Grace Paul (one of the kidnapped girls in Nigeria), my leaders, and so on. This is called, "quantum entanglement." The indigenous peoples of the world have known about this connection for thousands of years, but because our scientists could not prove it, we've lost a lot of ground over the past few decades.

Jesus said in the New Testament that we are all one. Let's call this "quantum spirituality."

It is hard to get our heads around the fact that what we do and say can impact the willow tree outside or that the willow tree, blowing in the wind, can impact our lives. We are superior beings, after all. That is our mind-set. I think we all know deep down that our actions can affect other humans and our environment but to what extent? I've listed some books in the "For Further Reading" chapter on this topic.

Name five people or events that your thoughts and actions have had an impact on.

Date:_____

_____

_____

_____

_____

What **negative** thoughts or actions have impacted other people or events? How and why were they impacted?

_____

_____

_____

_____

_____

_____

_____

_____

_____

_____

_____

> *Once you replace negative thoughts with positive ones, you'll start having positive results.*
>
> *—Willie Nelson*

What **positive** thoughts or actions have impacted other people or events? How and why were they impacted?

_____

_____

_____

_____

_____

_____

_____

_____

_____

_____

_____

_____

_____

> *What effect am I having on this world? I'm not sure yet. I have my worries, doubts, and fears, but the way I'm trying to affect the world is with positive, right action.*
>
> *—Robert Gossett*

Will you take any action based on your answers to the last two questions? What will you do? When will you do it? How will you do it? More importantly, will you be able to measure the impact of your actions?

Date:_____

_____

_____

_____

_____

_____

_____

_____

_____

_____

_____

If I send out positive messages, it will set a chain

of healthy thought processes.

—Persis Khambatta

Name five people or events your thoughts and actions **might** have an impact on. Examples might be the clerk at the grocery store, the librarian, the teller at the bank, and so forth.

Date:_____

_____

_____

_____

_____

What **negative** thoughts or actions of yours **might** impact these people or events? How? Why?

_____

_____

_____

_____

_____

_____

It takes but one positive thought when given a chance to survive and thrive to overpower an entire army of negative thoughts.

—Robert H. Schuller

What **positive** thoughts or actions of yours *might* impact these people or events? How? Why?

Date:_____

_____

_____

_____

_____

_____

_____

_____

_____

_____

_____

_____

_____

Will you take any action based on your answers to the previous two questions? What will you do? When will you do it? How will you do it? Most importantly, will you be able to measure the impact of your actions?

_____

_____

_____

_____

_____

_____

_____

_____

_____

_____

_____

_____

_____

_____

_____

> *There is no way a spirit of resistance that has sunk so*
>
> *deep in the population can be repressed.*
>
> *—Oliver Tambo*

Name five people or events you think your thoughts and actions will in *no way* impact. Examples might be your neighbor three streets over, your politicians, the owner of a business in town you have never visited, and so forth.

Date:_____

_____

_____

_____

_____

_____

What **negative** thoughts or actions of yours could impact the *no way* people or things? This will take some thought. Is there something you are doing that could impact them even indirectly? The point I am trying to help you see is that we are truly all connected. For example, if I don't take care of my septic system, could the bacteria seep into the water supply impacting my neighbor three streets away? If my yard is a total mess with trash everywhere, could that impact my neighbor three streets away? Every time he drives by he gets angry? See where I am going with this?

_____

_____

_____

What **positive** thoughts or actions of yours could impact the ***no way*** people or things? How? Why? For example, if I take care of my property by keeping it neat and clean, could it encourage my neighbor I do not know three streets away to keep his property neat and clean? This would generate a sense of respect for the community at large? We have actually seen this happen in the inner cities' housing neighborhoods.

Date:_____

_____

_____

_____

_____

_____

_____

_____

_____

_____

_____

_____

_____

_____

Will you take any action based on your answers to the previous two questions? What will you do? When will you do it? How will you do it? Most importantly, will you be able to measure the impact of your actions?

Date:_____

_____

_____

_____

_____

_____

_____

_____

_____

_____

_____

_____

_____

_____

_____

> *Hi, my name is Joan Marie. It is nice to meet you.*
>
> *What is your name?*
>
> *Joan Marie Gagnon*

A very dear friend of mine with lots of great ideas thought that something as simple as introducing yourself to someone and asking his or her name could contribute to world peace. My brother-in-law, Frank, did this often while in restaurants. The server would introduce herself, "Hi, I'm Jane, and I'll be your server today." Frank would then say, "Hi, I'm Frank, and this is my wife, Judy, my sister-in-law, Joan, and my brother-in-law, Jim." Everyone would crack up laughing, but we suddenly had a special connection to the server. Try it the next time you go out to a restaurant.

Can you think of other instances when introducing yourself to someone or asking someone's name might spark a more personal connection with him or her—a connection that would make the other person feel special, recognized, and appreciated?

Date:_____

_____

_____

_____

_____

_____

Chapter 3

Unconditional Love

About a year ago, I was reading one of my favorite kinds of books—usually self-help or self-improvement. It challenged me to describe *unconditional love*. Wow! That stopped me in my tracks. I did my best and described unconditional love as doing anything for the people I loved—my husband, children, siblings, parents, etc.—including jumping in front of a bus to save them, if it came down to that. Unconditional love meant I would do anything to protect my loved ones. Wikipedia says, "Unconditional love is known as affection without any limitations or love without conditions." [2]

Does unconditional love deplete the person who is giving it?

Date:_____

_____

_____

_____

_____

_____

Fr. Richard Rohr said "If unconditional love, loyalty, and obedience are the tickets to an eternal life, then my black Labrador, Venus, will surely be there long before me, along with all the dear animals in nature who care for their young at great cost to themselves and have suffered so much at the hands of humans." We've often heard of a dog's unconditional love. Most of us know what that means even if we have never owned a dog.

Knowing what unconditional love means to you is important because we are all connected. If we can experience unconditional love every minute of every day, the world has to feel it too. Once you experience unconditional love, you will want that experience daily.

So, what does unconditional love mean to you? Don't think about it too much. Write whatever comes to mind. We will continue to explore this throughout the chapter.

Date:_____

_____

_____

_____

_____

_____

_____

_____

_____

_____

Understanding *conditional* love may help. Think of conditional love as being *earned*. An example of conditional love might be you being expected to make others happy. They will love you with the condition that you continually make them happy. You may resent this or find it irritating or difficult.

Love should not be a power struggle. Many people take unusual measures to avoid love, never mind unconditional love. Yet the desire for unconditional love is what drives all of us in the grand scheme of things. Unconditional love should be given freely no matter how it impacts us.

Are there people in your life who give you **unconditional** love? Make a list.

Date: _____

_____

_____

_____

_____

_____

Are there people in your life who give you **conditional** love? Make a list.

Date:_____

_____

_____

_____

_____

_____

These can be difficult questions. You might be ready to jump to another chapter but wait! This was a tough chapter to write because of its intensity. In fact, I thought I had finished the book but while proofreading, I realized this chapter was barely finished. I had been quick to move on too.

Why are we exploring this topic? When I pursued this idea of unconditional love and world peace, it became apparent from my research that before we can give unconditional love, we must experience unconditional love for ourselves. It makes so much sense, right? But how many people in the world *have* experienced it? My guess would be a small percentage. Therefore, we have a lot of work to do, so don't give up.

> Simply put, love is the answer to
>
> every challenge that you face.
>
> —Hilarion

If love is the answer to every challenge we face, then it only stands to reason that love is the answer to every challenge our world faces. Neuroscience has proven that loving ourselves can change our DNA. It has also proven that human DNA can change and rearrange photons in the universe. Photons are light particles, which are the building blocks of our world. For more information on this subject, I highly recommend watching scientist Gregg Braden's YouTube videos on this matter. He is listed in the "For Further Reading" chapter.

Let's do some work on loving ourselves unconditionally. As Jesus said, "Physician, heal thyself" (Luke 4:23).

Are there things about yourself that you continually criticize? List them. Beside each item, indicate if you feel it is possible to stop beating yourself up regarding that issue. How will you do this?

Date:_____

_____

_____

Additional reading of Dr. Joe Dispenza's books would be extremely beneficial in this area. I especially like *Breaking the Habit of Being Yourself.*

Now, I want you to brag about yourself. Write a list of things that make you feel proud of yourself. You don't have to brag to everyone. Just brag about yourself in this journal.

Date:_____

_____

_____

_____

_____

_____

_____

_____

_____

Are you taking care of yourself physically? Small steps in this area can make a huge difference in your self-love. What five things can you do to get to a better you physically? You might think this contradicts not criticizing yourself, but it does not. We all know what we need to do to be healthier.

Date:_____

_____

_____

_____

_____

_____

Are you always running around because of a crazy schedule? What if you gave yourself the gift of time? Can you make some time each day or each week for yourself? If you can, what will you do with this time?

_____

_____

_____

_____

_____

Design a positive affirmation you can say to yourself daily. You can repeat it anywhere and anytime to yourself.

Date:_____

_____

_____

_____

_____

_____

The modern teaching now is to live in the present moment. I struggle with that a lot. Here is how I interpret it for myself. When I find myself thinking of the past or the future, I try to focus on what is happening right now. It helps keep me from worrying about the future and thinking of how I could have done things differently in the past. I have no control over either but trying to control the future and change the past can bring in a lot of negativity. It is powerful if you can spot the negativity when it first starts. Then you can jump to positive affirmations.

Do you think you need to see a therapist? Many people believe it is a sign of weakness to go to a therapist. On the contrary, it is a sign of strength. What are your thoughts on this matter? Would you consider giving it a try? Why or why not?

Date:_____

_____

_____

_____

_____

_____

I mentioned to you earlier that my definition of unconditional love was to do anything for a loved one, even if it meant stepping in front of a bus to save that person. About a year after I had asked myself what I thought unconditional love was, I experienced it.

I was volunteering at an eye clinic in Mexico, which was run by members of a Texas rotary club. I was apprehensive about doing this because I am not in the medical field and have never done well with the sight of someone else's blood. However, this was my husband's second trip, and I thought it would be awesome to experience this journey with him.

I was asked to work in the operating room where they removed cataracts, but I knew that I'd end up being a casualty and that it wasn't a good fit. So I was reassigned to pre-op. In pre-op, my job was to put eye drops in the patients' eyes, wash their faces with an antiseptic, give them a Tylenol PM, and have them wash their hands with a sanitizer.

As I was washing one elderly gentleman's face, a sudden rush of peace came over me. It kept happening as I washed each patient's face. I have never experienced this feeling before. I mentioned it to one of my fellow volunteers, and she said she thought I had felt God's presence. "Really?" I said. Then I started to think that maybe that feeling was unconditional love. Yes, I would have jumped in front of a bus to save each one of those patients.

My hope was to experience this feeling of peace every day. It doesn't seem to happen automatically. I must consciously remember that special feeling of peace and bring it on demand. This is a lifelong process. Being able to somehow bottle it would be wonderful.

Chapter 4

Forgiveness

> Holding onto anger is like grasping a hot coal with
>
> the intent of throwing it at someone else;
>
> you are the one who gets burned.
>
> —Buddha

Forgiving someone who has done you or your family a wrong can be tough. Forgiveness, whether it is for us or for others, may be the lynchpin to a more peaceful world.

I dislike chain letters, but wouldn't it be wonderful if you forgave five people and asked them to forgive five people with the intent of keeping the forgiveness going around the world? This would certainly have an impact on bringing about a more peaceful world.

Hold on, though. Just what does true forgiveness mean? It means truly letting go of all anger and negative thoughts toward the other person or situation. It must come from deep within your core. It is a state of mind and a state of loving forgiveness. Just the words, "I forgive you," do not constitute forgiveness. Hmmm, this certainly is not easy. It may take several tries before you get it right.

To top it off, the person you are forgiving does not need to apologize to you. That is not what is important. Forgiveness does not condone what someone else has done or pretend something never happened. Keep in mind, too, you do not have to tell the person that you forgive him or her.

Forgiving others has significant health benefits besides making the world a more peaceful place. Scientists say it improves the health of those who forgive and those receiving forgiveness. If you think about it, holding a grudge causes us more pain than it causes the person with whom we are angry, right? Some of the health benefits of forgiving are lower blood pressure, reduced pain, healthier hearts, reduced stress, and, even extended lives.

It seems like this chapter is a long one. As I was writing the book, I kept coming back to add things to this chapter. Personally, I had a lot of work to do on this subject, and many issues continually came up. Anyway, let's get to it.

Name five people you need to forgive. You don't have to forgive them just yet but list their names.

Date:_____

_____

_____

_____

_____

> **The weak can never forgive.**
>
> **Forgiveness is the attribute of the strong.**
>
> **—Mahatma Gandhi**

Name five colossal mistakes others have made that you might be able to forgive.

Date:_____

_____

_____

_____

_____

_____

> **Mistakes are always forgivable,**
>
> **if one has the courage to admit them.**
>
> **—Bruce Lee**

What five colossal mistakes have you made in your life for which you would love to be forgiven?

Date:_____

_____

_____

_____

_____

Name five small mistakes others have made that you might be able to forgive.

Date:_____

_____

_____

_____

_____

_____

What are five small mistakes you have made for which you would love to be forgiven?

Date:_____

_____

_____

_____

_____

Stages of Forgiveness

There are several stages of forgiveness. Let's walk through this together.

Choose one person from your colossal mistake list of people on page 35 to forgive.

Be specific. Who hurt you? When? Where?

Date:_____

_____

_____

_____

_____

What did they do to hurt you or your family? At this time, try not to hate the person but hate the act or the issue. It is important not to hate the person.

Date:_____

_____

_____

_____

_____

_____

What feelings and emotions arise when you think about this (betrayal, disgust, sadness)?

Date:_____

_____

_____

_____

_____

_____

Do you feel a sense of power over this individual? Are you maintaining control over that person by refusing to forgive him or her? Acknowledging this is important. In the end, it only hurts you to continue this hate and grudge.

Date:_____

_____

_____

_____

_____

_____

Is there any way you can rationalize a reason this happened? Can you empathize with that person? Remember, though, you are not condoning what happened. These are tough questions.

Date:_____

_____

_____

_____

_____

Would you like to get revenge? Revenge is not worth the effort, but sometimes it helps us heal if we think about it but don't act upon it. Can you see how it might potentially hurt many others around you?

Date:_____

_____

_____

_____

_____

_____

_____

Do you want a future with this vengefulness? Whom is it going to hurt? Whom will it benefit?

Date:_____

_____

_____

_____

_____

_____

It is important to know that your anger may come and go for months and even years. If you go through this process of answering the above questions each time, it will become less and less difficult until you realize that it is not worth it anymore.

It is a good idea to take a break between individuals when you will go through this process for several people you want to forgive. It can be a very draining and an emotional time. I recommend that you treat this time as being very special and when it is over, leave the emotion in that moment. Walk out of the room feeling refreshed and not drained.

How will you forgive that person? Will you forgive him or her in person? Will you forgive him or her within yourself? Each situation is different, and you will have to determine whether dragging the topic up to that person will cause more harm or good. I do believe that if you forgive that person within yourself, he or she will know it somehow. I don't necessarily feel it is critical to tell that individual to his or her face. But again, it may solidify the forgiveness for you.

What is your plan and why do you want to handle it this way?

Date: _____

_____

A good way to end this session is to write down five people or things for which you are grateful.

Date:_____

_____

_____

_____

_____

_____

Forgive Yourself

> It's almost like peeling an onion. Layer by layer, forgiving others,
>
> you really do get to the point where you can forgive yourself.
>
> —Patty Duke

It is thought that we cannot forgive others until we forgive ourselves, and we cannot forgive ourselves until we forgive others. Forgiving ourselves can be harder than forgiving others. Once you begin to forgive yourself, you open yourself up to unconditional love. This forgiveness will radiate out into the universe and touch many people you don't even know.

> You have the power to be miserable the rest of your life.
>
> —Dr. Phil

Now, go back to page 36 to select one colossal mistake or action for which you would like to forgive yourself. Let's go through the process together so you can reach a point where you might be able to forgive yourself. It is important to note, too, that this *is* a process, and you may need to repeat this process several times on this one issue. You may only get through part of this process. The point is to persevere until you have reached forgiveness. It can happen.

Be specific. Describe the mistake. Did you hurt someone? Who? When? Where?

Date:_____

_____

_____

_____

_____

How did you hurt this person or people? At this time, try not to be angry with yourself but hate the act or the issue. It is important not to hate yourself or to be angry with yourself.

Date:_____

_____

_____

_____

_____

What feelings and emotions arise when you think about this (betrayal, disgust, sadness)?

Date:_____

_____

_____

_____

_____

_____

Is your punishment not forgiving yourself? Are you keeping this issue alive in yourself for a reason? Acknowledging this is important. In the end, it only hurts you to maintain this hate and punishment.

Can you rationalize why this happened? Not that you are condoning your actions, but can you explain why this might have happened? Don't beat yourself up anymore.

Date:_____

_____

_____

_____

_____

Would you like to pay for your actions? Have you already paid for them somehow? In ancient times, a sacrifice was made for forgiveness. Can you make a sacrifice now or give back somehow to pay for your mistake? Do you think that would help alleviate your guilt and sadness?

Date:_____

_____

_____

_____

_____

_____

_____

_____

_____

_____

Do you want your future to have this guilt or sadness? Whom is it going to hurt? Whom will it benefit?

Date:_____

_____

_____

_____

_____

Saying I'm Sorry - Is it important for you to say you are sorry to someone? Will it just make matters worse by bringing the issue up again? Will forgiving yourself be enough? Every situation is different, and you need to be prepared for that person to not be ready to forgive you. On the other hand, apologizing to someone may open up a lifetime of love for which you have been dreaming. What is your plan?

Date:_____

_____

_____

_____

_____

_____

_____

_____

_____

_____

_____

_____

_____

_____

_____

_____

It is critical to know that your emotions may come and go for months and even years around this issue. If you go through this process each time, it will become less and less painful until you realize that it is not beneficial to continue to beat yourself up.

It is probably better to spread out the sessions when you go through this process of self-forgiveness. It can be a very draining and an emotional time. I recommend that you treat this time as being very special and when your journaling time is over, leave the emotion in that moment. Walk out of the room feeling refreshed and not drained.

A good way to end this session is to write down five people or things for which you are grateful.

Date:_____

_____

_____

_____

_____

_____

_____

Chapter 5

That Guy Who Just Cut You Off

> Life is 10% what happens to you and
>
> 90% how you react to it.
>
> —Charles R. Swindoll

Anger

Most of us have probably experienced a person cutting in front of us while driving or in line at the grocery store. I think as I have aged and mellowed a bit, I don't sweat the small stuff—or do I?

I have to admit that some days other people's inconsiderateness bothers me. Do their actions get me angry or is there something else going on? Maybe my pent-up anger erupts when these *small* actions occur, and I overreact.

Dr. Joe Dispenza, during a lecture on YouTube, said, "If you want world peace, you better not be mad at anyone or hate anyone." That hit home with me. His point was that we are all connected. This means that my angry thought about so and so has an impact on everyone.

An angry world is not a peaceful world. That is for certain. How can we ever possibly have a peaceful world when so many angry people live in it? It is very overwhelming. There is so much anger and anxiety in the world relating to politics and power, how can we change this?

I believe we just need to take one step at a time. The fact that you picked up this book and have gotten this far is encouraging for the future of world peace. Every inner negative emotion we can turn into a positive one builds peace in the world. Do not be discouraged.

Angry outbursts can be healthy and normal, too, as long as they don't hurt anyone else or get out of control. I don't believe we can ever eliminate anger. Sometimes anger can spur us on to better things and make change happen. Life is filled with events we cannot control that cause anger. It may even be justifiable outrage. The bottom line is how we handle it.

Many spiritual leaders, coaches, and counselors encourage their clients to focus on happiness without recognizing their anger. Stuff the anger away somewhere. I believe this is wrong. We need to address our anger as well as what makes us happy.

Can you think of five issues that make you angry?

Date:_____

_____

_____

_____

_____

Can you think of ways to take that anger and turn it into a positive emotion?

_____

_____

_____

_____

> Anybody can become angry—that is easy, but to be mad at
> the right person and to the right degree and at the right
> time and for the right purpose, and in the right way—
> that is not within everybody's power and is not easy.
>
> —Aristotle

An episode of yelling or screaming in an empty house or hitting a pillow over and over can bring a lot of pent-up anger out of you before you turn it inward or outward on others.

Here are some questions that might determine if you have some pent-up anger:

- Are you impatient with others?
- Do you criticize others?
- Do you belittle others and put them down?
- Do you have a short temper?
- Do you blame everyone else?
- Are you irritable?
- Do people avoid you?
- Do you withdraw from people?
- Are you a Dr. Jekyll that turns into a Mr. Hyde?

Do any of these questions resonate with you? I know it's hard to face sometimes.

Date:_____

_____

_____

_____

_____

The most difficult part of this exercise is coming face-to-face with the fact that you may have anger issues. Maybe the anger isn't full-blown rage, but most people have some anger pent up. Many of us have been taught not to show our feelings so we may not recognize pent-up anger. Anger can mask other issues such as fear, anxiety, sadness, insecurity, shame, hurt, or guilt. These anger issues can go way back to childhood.

This book is not meant to be intense therapy, but it may help you realize that small steps toward change can benefit you or that you, in fact, need some professional help. I think we all need professional help throughout our lives.

What do you think could be causing your anger issues?

Date:_____

_____

_____

_____

_____

Our uncontrolled or suppressed anger can have an impact on our global neighbors. Can you relate to this? Please write your positive and negative thoughts about your anger's impact on world peace.

_____

_____

_____

_____

> For every minute you remain angry, you give
>
> up sixty seconds of peace of mind.
>
> —Ralph Waldo Emerson

Here is an example of some of my anger and what I am doing about it. I am furious at our politicians in the United States as well as other world leaders. I realize that being angry doesn't help unless I somehow turn it into positive energy. So every morning when I meditate, I visualize myself giving the President a big hug and then send him all the love I can. I do that with President al-Assad of Syria too. I am also on a letter-writing campaign to my government representatives at all levels. We can't just vote and walk away as in the past. I feel better just typing this.

Happiness

> Happiness is not something you postpone for the future;
>
> it is something you design for the present.
>
> —Jim Rohn

What are five things that make you happy?

Date: _____

_____

_____

_____

_____

_____

Was there a time in your life when you were truly happy? How old were you? Was it for an extended period or just a day or so? Who else was involved? Where did you live? Did where you live play a role in your happiness? Describe this time of happiness in as much detail as possible.

_____

_____

_____

_____

_____

_____

Do you think your happiness level impacts those around you? How?

_____

_____

_____

_____

_____

Can you name five people who are truly happy? What do you think is their secret? If you can, ask them and then come back to this page to write their answers?

Date:_____

_____

_____

_____

_____

_____

_____

_____

_____

_____

> I'm afraid of happy people.
>
> They're chemically unbalanced.
>
> —Shirley Manson

Have you ever been with a group of people that all seemed to be happy and joking and then someone who was angry or sad walked in and changed the whole tenor of the group? I'm sure we can all relate to that experience.

And then on the other spectrum, have you ever been in a group where everyone was grumpy and gloomy, and then a happy person walked in and everyone perked up?

It isn't realistic to think we can always be happy, but can you see how it has an impact on you and those you touch? Now, if you believe that your happiness transcends to many individuals, should that not be our goal?

Will happy people make a more peaceful world?

_____

_____

_____

_____

_____

If we all concentrated on doing things that made us happy, the world would be a different place. *We* would be different. Start now by making one of your goals to be happy. This means you will spend less time on goals that don't make you happy. It is very logical, right? For example, spending time on goals to make lots of money and achieve success do not always bring happiness.

Studies are now popping up indicating that happiness is great for the heart, lengthens the lifespan, fights illnesses, strengthens the immune system, reduces stress, and helps our bodies have fewer aches and pains. Hmmm, can't beat that. It's just the opposite of what anger produces for our bodies.

List some simple things to do that will make you happy such as watching the sunrise and the sunset, walking in nature, playing golf, and babysitting grandkids.

_____

_____

_____

_____

_____

Who benefits from your happiness besides the obvious? (Think outside the box)

_____

_____

_____

_____

_____

Knowing there are things and situations in your life that do not make you happy, do you think you could make some significant changes to get yourself into newer situations that would make you happy? If so, describe them. If there is nothing you can change, why?

_____

_____

_____

> **Success is not the key to happiness. Happiness is the key to success.**
>
> **If you love what you are doing, you will be successful.**
>
> **—Albert Schweitzer**

Pretend you have no limitations at all. Write a story about a change you want to make that would bring you happiness. Include as much detail as possible: what, how, when, where, etc. It is okay if it is fiction. If you keep a positive spin on your thoughts, synchronicity might seep into the equation.

_____

_____

_____

_____

_____

_____

_____

_____

_____

_____

_____

_____

For the sake of world peace, do you feel you could make your goals happy oriented and continually work on those goals? Now that you have spent time on happiness, please go to Sticky Note Journaling, Week 2, found on page 119. Keep the happiness quotient in play at all times.

Chapter 6

The Root of All Evil

> Money is the root of all evil, and yet it is
>
> such a useful root that we cannot get on without it
>
> any more than we can without potatoes.
>
> —Louisa May Alcott

I have heard most of my life that money was the root of all evil. Is money the root cause of all our world conflicts or is it the seeking of power? What is your opinion on the root of all evil?

Date:_____

_____

_____

_____

_____

Whatever your opinion is regarding the root of all evil, there is probably a good and a bad aspect to the root. For example, there are positive and negative sides to money. Therefore, is money neutral in reality? It is the person and energy behind the money that matters.

Can you see the positives and negatives in your answer to what the root of all evil is? Explain each side.

Date: _____

_____

_____

_____

_____

_____

Do you see yourself or others exhibiting negative aspects of what you think the root of all evil is that could impact others and consequently, world peace? What can you do to turn this into a positive, no matter how small it is?

Date:_____

_____

_____

_____

_____

_____

_____

_____

Chapter 7

The Letters

> Letters are something from you. It's a different
>
> kind of intention than writing an e-mail.
>
> —Keanu Reeves

Over the years, I have written many letters to others and to myself, but they never got mailed. It is a form of journaling that I especially like. Because I know the letters will not be sent, I can say whatever is on my mind, come up with interesting solutions to problems, and complain about this or that. It is very cleansing. I usually burn the letters though.

Lately, I have taken to writing letters of appreciation to people in my life and even people that are not in my circle like the President, the Governor, and so on. That too has been very freeing and liberating. I no longer feel like a slave with no say in my future.

Coming up in this chapter, I have suggested various people to whom you should write handwritten letters. If you can, make it a habit of writing these letters on a monthly basis to the same people or to different people.

Today, write a letter to someone you love very much. It can be a spouse, partner, child, sibling, or anyone else that you want to express your love to. Expressing love with the written word is incredibly powerful. You can choose to mail this letter, file it, or burn it. Even if you do not mail it, the loved one will feel it in his or her heart and soul.

Date:_____

Developing compassion for Congress and politicians is

a good way to begin practicing the new social activism

if you want to make effective changes in the world.

Perhaps the most startling new insight of all is that there

is no other way to effectively change the world.

—Gary Zukav

The above quote may be hard for some to swallow. Many politicians run for office because they truly want to serve the people and make the lives of citizens better. I have learned from discussions I have had with local politicians that they never hear from their constituents. They love getting letters from us. In only one instance did I write a letter and not get a response back from the politician.

What five politicians or leaders would you be willing to write letters to, outlining your concerns about peace?

_____

_____

_____

_____

_____

_____

Today, select one of those people to write a letter to, discussing your concern about peace, whether it is a local, national, or international issue. It is important to thank that person for his or her service even if you don't agree with his or her ideas. Most of these leaders never hear "thank-you". You can choose to mail it or not to mail it.

Date: _____

_____

_____

_____

_____

_____

_____

_____

_____

_____

_____

_____

_____

_____

_____

> **To write is human, to receive a letter: Divine!**
>
> **—Susan Lendroth**

Today, take a stab at writing a letter to yourself. This is not an easy thing to do, but it is critical in your commitment to taking steps that will promote a peaceful world. What have you learned about yourself since opening this book? What specific actions (small or large) will you take to bring peace to the world? What are your feelings about a peaceful world? Is it possible?

Date:_____

_____

_____

_____

_____

_____

_____

_____

_____

_____

_____

_____

Chapter 8

The Earth

> The planet will survive. Whether we get to be here and enjoy
>
> it, or enjoy life as we've known it, is what's questionable.
>
> —Ted Danson

When we think of a peaceful world, most of us think of no war or conflict. But there is another element. Our planet is in need of peace. Whether you believe in global warming or not, it is hard to ignore that the human race is slowly destroying our beautiful planet and its resources.

Name five issues of concern you have for our planet.

Date:_____

_____

_____

_____

_____

_____

One issue that bothers me greatly is the garbage that is floating in the Pacific Ocean. I recently did some research, while writing this book, on the Pacific

Ocean Garbage Patch. The patch consists mostly of tiny pepper-sized pieces as well as larger pieces of plastic. There seem to be conflicting reports as to the severity of this patch and the consequences. Needless to say, it is not a good situation. Scientists do not yet know what this is doing to the fish and the environment.

In my opinion, we don't have to be scientists to figure it out. We are continually impoverishing our planet and depleting it of its resources. Again, there is no need to be a scientist to realize the harm we are doing.

Is there any change you can make to your lifestyle that would help with your concerns for the earth? Even though our contribution is small, every effort is worth a million.

_____

_____

_____

_____

_____

Is there an issue you could address to your politicians or even the newspapers?

_____

_____

_____

_____

Is there a local environmental issue you and your neighbors could take action to remedy? For example, with your kids and grandkids pick up trash along the roads near your home.

Chapter 9

The Children

> Each generation imagines itself to be more intelligent
>
> than the one that went before it, and wiser
>
> than the one that comes after it.
>
> —George Orwell

There is a lot of confusion around the actual beginning and ending dates for the different generations. Therefore, the dates I used are approximate.

Some believe that millennials will save our planet. Millennials were born between 1980–1994. They are like the hippies of the sixties. They care about the environment and despise war. Millennials are very accepting of people, more informed, and more connected to the world. They are nonconformists, have very high standards, and hate consumerism. If this is true, it sounds like the rest of us have a good team coming behind us.

The millennials you know today (2017) are between the ages of twenty-three and thirty-seven. Can you list five millennials who have the previously listed traits?

_____

_____

_____

_____

_____

If you are from an earlier generation, can you support these millennials' ideals in some way? Describe how.

_____

_____

_____

_____

The generation born between 1995 and 2012– are called Gen Zs. They appear to be similar to the baby boomer generation (1945-1964). They are realistic, pragmatic, and very competitive, but they also have many characteristics of the Gen Xs (1965-1979), which are environmentally aware and tech savvy. They also share the traits of the millennials in that they are very individualistic.

The Gen Zs you know today (2017) are twenty-two years old and younger. Can you list five Gen Zs? Do they have the previously listed traits?

_____

_____

_____

_____

If you come from an earlier generation, can you support these Gen Zs' ideals in some way? Describe how.

_____

_____

_____

_____

_____

Of course, not everyone fits nicely into a category, which probably would not be a good thing. The goal of this chapter is to help each older generation support the younger generations' ideals when it benefits world peace.

What do you observe about younger people as it relates to world peace?

_____

_____

_____

_____

_____

Many schools are now offering programs that bring about peace and mindfulness to help combat bullying and other violent actions. Schools in New York City and in other districts are now teaching yoga and meditation.

There is much online data and information about these programs. I encourage you to research whether your local schools offer these programs or not. If not, what steps might you take to promote these programs?

_____

_____

_____

_____

_____

Are there civic groups like the Rotary Club, Lions Club, Boy Scouts and Girl Scouts, and YMCA, which may offer peace programs for youth in your area?

_____

_____

_____

_____

You may have children, grandchildren, great-grandchildren, nieces, and nephews who would benefit from programs regarding living in a peaceful world.

Describe the world you want for _our children_ and the ideas you have to make that a reality. Let's give them every tool to bring peace to their lives and humanity.

_____

_____

_____

_____

_____

_____

_____

Chapter 10

Reflections

As you move through the various chapters, you may need extra space to reflect on something that has touched your heart or being. I have provided additional lines for each chapter.

Chapter 1: The Power of Journaling

Date:_____

_____

_____

_____

_____

_____

_____

_____

_____

Chapter 2: I'm Connected to You?

Date:_____

_____

_____

_____

_____

_____

_____

_____

_____

_____

_____

_____

_____

_____

_____

_____

_____

_____

_____

_____

Chapter 3: Unconditional Love

Date:_____

_____

_____

_____

_____

_____

_____

_____

_____

_____

_____

_____

_____

_____

_____

_____

_____

_____

Chapter 4: Forgiveness

Date:_____

_____

_____

_____

_____

_____

_____

_____

_____

_____

_____

_____

_____

_____

_____

_____

_____

_____

_____

Chapter 5: That Guy Who Just Cut You Off

Date:_____

_____

_____

_____

_____

_____

_____

_____

_____

_____

_____

_____

_____

_____

_____

_____

_____

_____

Chapter 6: The Root of All Evil

Date:_____

_____

_____

_____

_____

_____

_____

_____

_____

_____

_____

_____

_____

_____

_____

_____

_____

_____

_____

_____

Chapter 7: The Letters

Date:_____

_____

_____

_____

_____

_____

_____

_____

_____

_____

_____

_____

_____

_____

_____

_____

Chapter 8: The Earth

Date:_____

_____

_____

_____

_____

_____

_____

_____

_____

_____

_____

_____

_____

_____

_____

_____

_____

_____

_____

Chapter 9: The Children

Date:_____

Chapter 11

Journaling Exercises/Meditations

Sticky Note Journaling

Introduction

Each week will have a theme. Each day you will write your answers to that week's theme question on a sticky note, napkin, corner of the newspaper, or whatever works but preferably a sticky note pad. The answers should be simple—just one or two words. It's doable, right?

Since journaling can be somewhat personal, you can choose to keep the sticky notes, post them on your bathroom mirror or refrigerator, or rip them to shreds. Also, you do not have to take any action after you complete each day's question unless that is your desire. Does this sound more appealing?

Sticky Note Journaling, Week One

Okay, it is week one of the Sticky Note Journaling Series. This week your goal is to write five things for which you are grateful, every day, on one sticky note. It can be as simple as a great cup of coffee for breakfast or something more complex. Don't think too much about it. Just let it flow. So, at the end of the week, you could potentially have thirty-five things for which you are grateful. Oh, you can repeat things from previous days. You can choose to keep the sticky note or tear it to shreds.

Here is a fantastic article on scientifically proven benefits of expressing gratitude.

From *Psychology Today*: **7 Scientifically Proven Benefits of Gratitude, Amy Morin, Psychotherapist, April 3, 2015.**[3]

https://www.psychologytoday.com/blog/what-mentally-strong-people-dont-do/201504/7-scientifically-proven-benefits-gratitude

Sticky Note Journaling, Week Two

It is week two of the Sticky Note Journaling Series. This week write one goal you want to accomplish in the next five years, every day, on one sticky note. It can be an easy accomplishment or something grandiose such as retiring in five years. Don't think too much about it. Just let it flow.

So, at the end of the week, you could potentially have seven goals you want to accomplish in the next five years. Try not to repeat a goal from the previous day, but, hey, it is your journal. If a goal is very important, it might keep recurring.

Once you have written this goal, be alert to the beginning of synchronicities. Per Wikipedia, synchronicity is a concept, which was first explained by the analytical psychologist Carl Jung. It holds that events are *meaningful coincidences* if they occur with no causal relationship yet seem to be meaningfully related. [4]

I will share with you a synchronicity that happened to me. A few years ago I had a goal of going to a foreign country where I could volunteer to help the people in need. I didn't have any expectations of the type of work I would do. I even had a picture of indigenous women on my vision board. About a week after I wrote the goal and made the vision board, I was talking to a friend from California about this goal. She yelled with excitement that she was going to Guatemala to work with the indigenous women in a small village on how to start a business. I signed up that day with no questions asked. I knew that was a synchronicity. But, it doesn't have to be big synchronicities. Be alert.

Dr. Joe Dispenza says, "Dare to ask for synchronicities related to your specific desired outcomes. So when events begin to occur in your life, you can choose to be a scientist in the process of discovery." I recommend you keep notes on any synchronicities that occur relating to these five-year goals. You can choose to keep the sticky note or tear it to shreds.

Sticky Note Journaling, Week Three

It is week three of the Sticky Note Journaling Series. This week your goal is to write five things that make you happy, every day, on one sticky note. If you could just work on making yourself happy, what would you do? Just let it flow. So, at the end of the week, you could potentially have thirty-five things that make you happy. You can repeat things from previous days. You can choose to keep the sticky note or tear it to shreds.

Here is a fantastic article in *Psychology Today*, "Why Pursuing Happiness Is the Greatest Goal," https://www.psychologytoday.com/blog/meditation-modern -life/201406/why-pursuing-happiness-is-the-greatest-goal[5]

Sticky Note Journaling, Week Four

It is week four of the Sticky Note Journaling Series. This week's theme is forgiveness. Although it might get a little deep for you, try to stick with it for the week.

Each day you will write one or more things you would like to forgive yourself for on one sticky note. It can be as little as eating a piece of chocolate yesterday or something much bigger. It can be something recent or thirty years ago.

Benefits of Forgiving Yourself

Forgiveness is a very powerful healer. We don't realize how we punish ourselves daily and the impact it has on our psyche, body, and relationships. Here is a link to an article from *Psychology Today*, "Forgiving Yourself," https://www.psychologytoday.com/blog/emotional-nourishment/201704/forgiving-yourself[6]

You can choose to keep the sticky note or tear it to shreds.

Sticky Note Journaling, Week Five

It is week five of the Sticky Note Journaling Series. There's two more to go! The theme this week is random thoughts. The goal will be to write down the first five thoughts that come to mind when you pick up your pen and sticky note. It should take less than two minutes. They can be hilarious, serious, sad, happy, or boring. It is a brain dump.

Sometimes when I do this exercise, I don't seem to have any thoughts for a couple of minutes. Supposedly, it is a good way to reset your brain. If this happens to you, it is a gift. Some people try for hours to clear their minds when they are meditating. You did it just by asking yourself, *What is my next thought?* If you want to, you can pick one thought and continue writing about it on a larger piece of paper or on multiple sticky notes.

At the end of the week, read through the sticky notes. Did you have any good ideas? Did you take any action on one or more of those random thoughts?

Benefits of a Brain Dump or Writing down Random Thoughts

David Allen, in his book *Getting Things Done,* [7] advocates doing a brain dump at least once a week. Having followed David for years, I try to do this weekly and have seen the benefits over and over. We have thousands of thoughts per day. How many good thoughts do we capture for our benefit?

You can check out David Allen's book or this article in *Lifehack*: *How to Do the Ultimate Brain Dump,* http://www.lifehack.org/articles/productivity/how-to-do-the-ultimate-brain-dump.html.[8]

You can choose to keep the sticky note or tear it to shreds.

Sticky Note Journaling, Week Six

Communicate is the theme of week six in the Sticky Note Journaling Series. Do you call your friends on a regular basis? Do you reach out via text, email, or message on Facebook? Do you find out what your friends are up to by checking their Facebook page? Each day this week, write one or more names of people you haven't spoken with in way too long on a sticky note. It doesn't mean you have to contact them. Just write their names. By the end of the week, you could potentially have seven friends you might contact soon. It can be a childhood friend or someone you met last week.

Importance of Friendships

Friendships are voluntary. There is no structure like a family relationship. Friendships also change as life moves on. Surveys show that maintaining friendships is important to your happiness. Check out this article in *The Atlantic*, "How Friendships Change in Adulthood." https://www.theatlantic.com/health/archive/2015/10/how-friendships-change-over-time-in-adulthood/411466//. [9]

You can choose to keep the sticky note or tear it to shreds.

Sticky Note Journaling, Week Seven

Congratulations! If you are reading this, there is a good chance you participated in the entire Sticky Note Journaling Series. The purpose of these weekly journaling exercises was to introduce you slowly to journaling. I hope you realize that journaling doesn't have to take a lot of your time. Journaling isn't just about writing. Journaling can open up your life with only five minutes per day. It is *your* time. I would love to hear some feedback on your experiences from the past six weeks. You can reach out to me a joan@journalyourwayto.com.

Each day this week, choose one of the six-week topics that touched you. Then expand on the theme for five minutes. You'll need a bigger piece of paper for this or several sticky notes. Set a time, if necessary. When you journal about a topic, ask yourself who, what, where, why, and when, and you will have enough material to fill a piece of paper.

Sticky Note Journaling Themes

The themes for the previous weeks were gratitude, life goals, happiness, forgiveness, random thoughts, and friendship.

Meditations

Litmus Test

The Litmus Test exercise is designed to give you a go-to process when you need to tap into your logical and emotional brain. I believe everyone has intuition and knows when a decision is or isn't right. But our and our family's egos, along with financial issues, can cloud the decision-making process. This exercise can be used for many different decisions that come up in your life. The Litmus Test will help you tap into that intuition at a moment's notice and serve you well throughout your life.

You will require a quiet space, free from all distractions. You can even record the exercise on your phone or another electronic device so you can keep your eyes closed. It is a guided exercise. Go outside and find a stone or a smooth object you can hold in one hand. You may have something in your home, like a marble, although connecting to the energy of the earth is preferred. A marble is the size you want.

Take several deep breaths. Write down your question or decision so it is very clear in your mind. Close your eyes and hold the smooth, round object in your hand. Take several deep breaths. Now I want you to think of a time when you experienced peacefulness and bliss by yourself, a time when you were "in the zone." Where were you, what were you doing, and when was it? How old were you? Keeping your eyes closed, recognize what physical sensations you feel in your body. Are you relaxed? Are you smiling? Do you have butterflies in your stomach?

Keep your eyes closed. Keep that physical sensation alive. You want to be able to recreate this feeling so it is important to remember the sensation. Now feel the stone or rock in your hand. Connect your blissful feeling with this rock.

Now think of your question or decision you are addressing today. How have your feelings changed? Are you maintaining that blissful state, or do you immediately go to a bad place?

If you are able to maintain the blissful state while thinking about this issue, you are probably on the right track. On the other hand, if you went to a bad place, then more work needs to be done on your decision process, or you need to abandon the decision completely.

As you utilize the Litmus Test, you will develop a keen sense of your intuition. Use this test to guide you in your life's decisions.

Date: _____

_____

_____

_____

_____

_____

_____

_____

_____

_____

_____

_____

A Walk in the Woods

Imagine you are walking up a trail in the forest that leads to the ocean. You stop to admire the waves hitting the rock formations off in the distance. It is so hard to continue because of the beauty and serenity of this vista. You don't want to turn around, but you don't want to go forward on the trail either. You are perfectly content right here and right now.

Look down the trail you have just walked. Recount the most important lessons you have gathered from your life experiences. Then look ahead on the trail. Are there lessons to learn as you go forward in life?

Date: _____

_____

_____

_____

_____

_____

_____

_____

_____

_____

_____

_____

For Further Reading

1. *The Health Benefits of Journaling* by Maud Purcell, LCSW, CEAP, originally published on PsychCentral.com on 17 May 2016, https://psychcentral.com/lib/the-health-benefits-of-journaling/.

2. *Breaking the Habit of Being Yourself: How to Lose Your Mind and Create a New One*, by Dr. Joe Dispensa.

3. *Resilience from the Heart: The Power to Thrive in Life's Extremes* by Gregg Braden.

4. *Falling Upward: A Spirituality of the Two Halves of Life* by Richard Rohr.

Notes

1. **PsychCentral.** *The Health Benefits of Journaling* by Maud Purcell, LCSW, CEAP, 2016. https://psychcentral.com/lib/the-health-benefits-of-journaling/

2. *Wikipedia, The Free Encyclopedia.* https://en.wikipedia.org/wiki/Unconditional_love

3. **Psychology Today.** *7 Scientifically Proven Benefits of Gratitude.* Amy Morin, Psychotherapist. April 3, 2015. https://www.psychologytoday.com/blog/what-mentally-strong-people-dont-do/201504/7-scientifically-proven-benefits-gratitude

4. *Wikipedia, The Free Encyclopedia.* https://en.wikipedia.org/wiki/Synchronicity

5. **Psychology Today.** *Why Pursuing Happiness Is The Greatest Goal.* June 2014. https://www.psychologytoday.com/blog/meditation-modern-life/201406/why-pursuing-happiness-is-the-greatest-goal

6. **Psychology Today.** *Forgiving Yourself.* April 2017. https://www.psychologytoday.com/blog/emotional-nourishment/201704/forgiving-yourself

7. *Getting Things Done: The Art of Stress-Free Productivity* by David Allen.

8. **Lifehack.** *How to Do the Ultimate Brain Dump.* http://www.lifehack.org/articles/productivity/how-to-do-the-ultimate-brain-dump.html

9. **The Atlantic.** *How Friendships Change in Adulthood.* October 22, 2015. https://www.theatlantic.com/health/archive/2015/10/how-friendships-change-over-time-in-adulthood/411466//

Printed in the United States
By Bookmasters